WORKBOOK

For

A Radical Awakening

Turn Pain into Power, Embrace Your Truth, Live Free

Geny Press

Workbook Purpose

This workbook is designed to provide reliable and precise information on the subject matter at hand. The intention of this publication is to offer insightful insights into the discussed issue. It's important to note that the publisher is not obligated to provide accounting services or recognized legal counsel, as described in the book's promotional materials. For professional or legal advice, individuals should refer to the Declaration of Principles endorsed by a committee from the American Bar Association and a Committee of Associations and Publishers.

Usage Restrictions

Liability and Responsibility

Table of content

How To Use This Workbook

Great Day!

This companion workbook is designed to accompany and amplify the concepts explored in the main book. It offers a structured approach to help you engage deeply with the material, reflect on key lessons, and apply them to your life. This guide will walk you through how to effectively utilize this workbook to enhance your learning experience.

Key Lessons:

Each chapter of the workbook corresponds to a chapter in the main book. Before you dive into the exercises, review the key lessons and main takeaways from the associated chapter in the main book. This will set the stage for your workbook journey and provide context for the self-reflection and evaluation exercises.

Self-Reflection Questions:

Within each chapter's section, you'll find self-reflection questions designed to encourage introspection and deeper understanding. Take your time to contemplate these questions and write down your responses. Use this space to explore your thoughts, feelings, and insights related to the chapter's content. Feel free to refer back to these reflections as you progress through the workbook.

Final Evaluation Questions:

At the end of each chapter, you'll encounter final evaluation questions. These questions are intended to help you consolidate your understanding of the material and assess your grasp of the key concepts. Challenge yourself to answer these questions thoroughly and thoughtfully. Your responses will serve as a valuable gauge of your progress and learning.

Getting Started:

1. Begin by reviewing the introduction of the workbook. This will provide you with an overview of the structure and purpose of the workbook.

2. Familiarize yourself with the layout of each chapter's section, which includes key lessons, self-reflection questions.

3. As you work through each chapter, use the provided space to jot down your thoughts, insights, and responses. This workbook is your personal canvas for exploration.

Progress at Your Pace:

Feel free to progress through the workbook at your own pace. Some exercises might resonate deeply and require more time, while others might be quicker to complete. The journey is yours, and the goal is to engage meaningfully with the content.

Enhance Your Learning:

- Consider discussing your reflections with others who are reading the main book. Sharing insights can lead to rich discussions and new perspectives.

- Create a dedicated space, like a journal or notebook, to capture your workbook responses and additional notes.

- Revisit your previous reflections and evaluations as you move through the workbook to see how your understanding evolves.

Make It Your Own:

This workbook is your tool for growth and exploration. Feel free to customize it to your preferences. Highlight key points, underline passages, and add your thoughts in the margins. Personalize the experience to maximize your learning journey.

Thank you for embarking on this journey with us. The exercises within this workbook are designed to empower you to internalize the book's concepts, reflect on their relevance to your life, and ultimately transform knowledge into action.

Happy learning and growing!

Overview

"A Radical Awakening: Turn Pain into Power, Embrace Your Truth, Live Free" is a transformative self-help book authored by Shefali Tsabary, known for her expertise in conscious parenting and personal development. Released in 2021, the book delves into profound concepts that guide readers on a journey of self-discovery, healing, and empowerment. Tsabary's insightful and compassionate approach encourages readers to embrace their inner truths, confront past wounds, and harness their pain as a catalyst for personal growth and empowerment.

The book is structured into several sections, each addressing a crucial aspect of personal transformation:

The Awakening: Tsabary sets the stage by discussing the concept of awakening, highlighting the importance of recognizing the need for change and embarking on a journey of self-realization. She emphasizes that the path to transformation begins with an open heart and mind, allowing individuals to question societal norms and expectations.

Embracing Your Truth: In this section, Tsabary encourages readers to confront their deepest truths, shedding societal masks and pretenses. She guides them through the process of identifying and embracing their authentic selves, unearthing suppressed emotions, and acknowledging their vulnerabilities.

From Pain to Power: Tsabary introduces the transformative idea of using pain and suffering as a catalyst for growth and empowerment. She discusses how embracing and understanding one's pain can lead to healing and personal strength. Through real-life anecdotes and practical exercises, she provides tools to navigate through pain and emerge stronger on the other side.

Reclaiming Relationships: Relationships are a central theme of the book. Tsabary explores how embracing one's authenticity can lead to more meaningful and fulfilling connections with others. She addresses the challenges of navigating relationships while undergoing personal transformation and offers guidance on setting boundaries, expressing needs, and fostering genuine connections.

Unmasking the Ego: Tsabary delves into the concept of the ego and its impact on our lives. She helps readers recognize how the ego influences their thoughts, behaviors, and decisions. By shedding light on the ego's mechanisms, she empowers readers to transcend its limitations and align their actions with their authentic selves.

Living a Liberated Life: In the final section, Tsabary provides a roadmap for living a liberated life. She discusses the importance of mindfulness, self-compassion, and self-care as ongoing practices. Through mindfulness techniques and reflective exercises, she guides readers in cultivating a sense of inner freedom and joy.

Throughout the book, Tsabary seamlessly weaves together psychological insights, spiritual wisdom, and practical exercises. Her writing style is empathetic and relatable, making complex concepts accessible to a wide range of readers. Drawing from her background as a clinical psychologist and her own personal experiences, she offers a compelling narrative that encourages readers to embark on a profound journey of self-discovery and empowerment.

"A Radical Awakening" is a powerful guide for individuals seeking to break free from societal constraints, confront their pain, and transform their lives. Tsabary's message is one of hope and empowerment, inviting readers to embrace their truths, turn their pain into power, and ultimately live a life aligned with their authentic selves.

Part One: ASLEEP IN THE MATRIX
Soul Erosion

Key Lessons

1. **Recognizing Suppression:** Understand that soul erosion occurs when you suppress your authentic self, needs, and emotions to conform to external expectations or societal norms.

2. **Impact of Denial:** Denying your true feelings and desires can lead to soul erosion, eroding your sense of self-worth and causing emotional turmoil.

3. **Deconstructing Conditioning:** Examine how societal conditioning and past experiences have contributed to your soul erosion. Unravel these layers to regain your authentic self.

4. **Listening to Intuition:** Tune into your intuition and inner voice. By honoring your instincts, you can identify instances of soul erosion and begin the journey to healing.

5. **Reclaiming Authenticity:** Embrace vulnerability and authenticity. Allow yourself to express your truth, even if it challenges societal norms, and start the process of soul healing.

Self Reflection Questions

Reflect on times when you've suppressed your authentic self. How can you recognize these instances and their impact on your well-being?

_____

_____

_____

_____

_____

_____

_____

_____

_____

_____

_____

_____

Consider the emotions you've denied or buried. How has this denial contributed to soul erosion and affected your sense of self-worth?

_____

_____

_____

_____

_____

_____

_____

_____

_____

_____

_____

_____

_____

_____

Think about your past conditioning. How can you deconstruct these influences to uncover your authentic self beneath the layers?

_____

_____

_____

_____

_____

_____

_____

_____

_____

_____

_____

_____

———

Reflect on your connection to your intuition. How can you listen more closely to your inner voice to identify areas of soul erosion and begin the healing process?

_____

_____

_____

_____

_____

_____

_____

_____

_____

_____

———

Consider your willingness to be authentic. How can you embrace vulnerability, express your truth, and initiate the journey to reclaiming your authentic self?

The Idea of That Woman

Key Lessons

1. **Embrace Your Authentic Self:** Understand that societal expectations often create an "ideal" version of womanhood. Embrace your true self, letting go of the need to conform to external standards.

2. **Challenge Stereotypes:** Recognize the harm in perpetuating stereotypes about women's roles and behaviors. Challenge these narratives and empower yourself to break free from limiting beliefs.

3. **Release the Need for Approval:** Understand that seeking external validation can hinder your growth. Let go of the need for approval from others and find validation within yourself.

4. **Define Your Worth:** Realize that your worth is not defined by conforming to societal standards of beauty or success. Define your worth on your own terms, based on your unique qualities and values.

5. **Embrace Liberation:** Embrace the idea of liberation from societal expectations. Embrace your multifaceted identity, free from the constraints of others' perceptions.

Self Reflection Questions

Reflect on your journey to authenticity. How can you actively embrace your true self and let go of societal pressures to conform?

_____

_____

_____

_____

_____

_____

_____

_____

_____

_____

_____

_____

_____

Consider the stereotypes you've encountered. How can you challenge and dismantle these narratives to empower yourself and other women?

_____

_____

_____

_____

_____

_____

_____

_____

_____

_____

_____

_____

_____

_____

_____

Think about seeking validation from external sources. How can you shift your focus towards self-validation and find empowerment from within?

_____

_____

_____

_____

_____

_____

_____

_____

_____

_____

_____

_____

_____

Reflect on your self-worth. How can you redefine your worth based on your unique qualities, rather than conforming to external standards?

_____

_____

_____

_____

_____

_____

_____

_____

_____

_____

_____

_____

Contemplate the idea of liberation from societal expectations. How can you actively embrace your freedom to define your identity and live authentically?

Do We Dare to Own Our Part?

Key Lessons

1. **Taking Responsibility:** Understand that personal growth requires owning your actions, choices, and their consequences. Acknowledge your role in situations, even when it's uncomfortable.

2. **Breaking Patterns:** Recognize that owning your part in conflicts or challenges helps break repetitive patterns. By acknowledging your contributions, you can create healthier dynamics.

3. **Self-Awareness:** Cultivate self-awareness to identify your behaviors and reactions. Understand that acknowledging your part requires a deeper understanding of your triggers and responses.

4. **Empowerment through Ownership:** Realize that owning your part is an empowering step towards change. Understand that it allows you to transform negative cycles into opportunities for growth.

5. **Compassionate Accountability:** Approach self-ownership with compassion rather than judgment. Understand that acknowledging your part doesn't mean blaming yourself; it's about growth and learning.

Self Reflection Questions

Reflect on recent situations. How can you actively take responsibility for your actions and choices, regardless of the outcome?

_____

_____

_____

_____

_____

_____

_____

_____

_____

_____

_____

_____

Consider repetitive patterns in your life. How can acknowledging your role in these patterns contribute to breaking free from them?

_____

_____

_____

_____

_____

_____

_____

_____

_____

_____

_____

_____

_____

_____

Think about your reactions in conflicts. How can cultivating self-awareness help you recognize your part and contribute to more constructive resolutions?

_____

_____

_____

_____

_____

_____

_____

_____

_____

_____

_____

_____

_____

Reflect on your journey towards change. How can owning your part empower you to transform challenges into catalysts for personal growth?

_____

_____

_____

_____

_____

_____

_____

_____

_____

_____

_____

Consider your inner dialogue when reflecting on your part. How can you approach self-ownership with kindness and self-compassion, fostering growth rather than self-blame?

Part Two: CONFRONTING THE SHADOW
The Many Faces of the Ego

Key Lessons

1. **Ego's Influence:** Understand that the ego is a powerful force that shapes perceptions, actions, and relationships. Recognize its impact on various aspects of your life.

2. **False Identification:** Acknowledge that the ego often leads to false identification with roles, labels, and external validation. Understand that these attachments can hinder your true self.

3. **Inner Dialogue:** Recognize the ego's role in creating negative self-talk and self-doubt. Understand that this inner dialogue can be transformed through self-awareness.

4. **Comparisons and Competition:** Understand that the ego thrives on comparisons and competition, often leading to feelings of inadequacy. Recognize how these tendencies affect your well-being.

5. **Embracing Authenticity:** Realize that breaking free from the ego's grip requires embracing your authentic self. Understand that by doing so, you can experience true liberation.

Self Reflection Questions

Reflect on your daily thoughts and actions. How can you identify instances where the ego's influence shapes your perceptions and choices?

_____

_____

_____

_____

_____

_____

_____

_____

_____

_____

_____

_____

Consider the roles and labels you identify with. How can you detach from these attachments and cultivate a truer sense of self?

_____

_____

_____

_____

_____

_____

_____

_____

_____

_____

_____

_____

_____

Think about your inner dialogue. How can you become more aware of ego-driven negative self-talk and replace it with more empowering thoughts?

_____

_____

_____

_____

_____

_____

_____

_____

_____

_____

_____

Reflect on your tendencies to compare yourself to others. How can you recognize the ego's role in fostering competition and shift towards self-compassion?

_____

_____

_____

_____

_____

_____

_____

_____

_____

_____

_____

Consider your journey to authenticity. How can you actively work towards embracing your authentic self and experiencing the liberation that comes with it?

The Controllers

Key Lessons

1. **Identifying Control Patterns:** Understand that controllers are patterns of behavior driven by fear and the need for security. Recognize how these patterns manifest in various aspects of your life.

2. **Letting Go of Control:** Acknowledge that excessive control can lead to stress and resistance. Understand that letting go of the need to control every situation can bring freedom and peace.

3. **Trusting the Flow:** Realize that relinquishing control involves trusting the natural flow of life. Understand that surrendering to the unknown can lead to unexpected growth and opportunities.

4. **Releasing Fear:** Controllers often arise from fear of the unknown. Understand that facing and releasing these fears can help you break free from controlling behaviors.

5. **Embracing Flexibility:** Recognize that life is inherently uncertain. Embrace flexibility and adaptability as tools to navigate challenges with grace and resilience.

Self Reflection Questions

Reflect on your behaviors in various situations. How can you identify instances where controllers emerge as responses to fear and insecurity?

_____

_____

_____

_____

_____

_____

_____

_____

_____

_____

_____

_____

Consider areas where you seek excessive control. How can you recognize the toll it takes on your well-being and embrace the freedom of letting go?

_____

_____

_____

_____

_____

_____

_____

_____

_____

_____

_____

_____

_____

_____

_____

Think about trust in the unknown. How can you cultivate the courage to surrender control and trust the natural flow of life?

_____

_____

_____

_____

_____

_____

_____

_____

_____

_____

_____

———

Reflect on your fears that drive controlling behaviors. How can you confront and release these fears to break free from patterns of control?

———

———

———

———

———

———

———

———

———

———

———

———

———

Consider your reactions to uncertainty. How can you shift towards a mindset of flexibility and adaptability, allowing you to navigate challenges more effectively?

The Takers

Key Lessons

1. **Understanding Taker Dynamics:** Recognize that takers are individuals who drain your energy and exploit your generosity. Understand the dynamics that fuel these relationships.
2. **Boundary Setting:** Acknowledge the importance of setting healthy boundaries with takers. Understand that doing so preserves your energy and well-being.
3. **Self-Worth and Takers:** Realize that attracting takers can stem from low self-worth. Understand that valuing yourself and your needs can help you avoid such relationships.
4. **Guilt and Obligation:** Recognize the tendency to feel guilt or obligation when dealing with takers. Comprehend that focusing on your prosperity isn't egotistical, yet fundamental.
5. **Choosing Empowerment:** Understand that you have the power to choose the relationships you engage in. Recognize that surrounding yourself with supportive individuals is a form of self-care.

Self Reflection Questions

Reflect on your relationships. How can you identify instances where you've encountered takers and the impact they've had on your energy?

_____

_____

_____

_____

_____

_____

_____

_____

_____

_____

_____

_____

_____

Consider your boundaries with others. How can you actively set and maintain boundaries to protect your energy and well-being?

_____

_____

_____

_____

_____

_____

_____

_____

_____

_____

_____

_____

_____

_____

Think about your self-worth. How can valuing yourself and your needs lead you away from relationships with takers?

_____

_____

_____

_____

_____

_____

_____

_____

_____

_____

_____

_____

Reflect on guilt and obligation in relationships. How can you shift towards prioritizing your well-being without feeling guilty for asserting your needs?

Consider your circle of relationships. How can you empower yourself by choosing to surround yourself with individuals who support and uplift you?

Part Three: BACK TO NATURE
Nature's Design of Our Body

Key Lessons

1. **Intelligent Design:** Understand that your body is intelligently designed by nature to function optimally. Recognize the complexity and interconnectedness of its systems.

2. **Self-Healing Mechanisms:** Acknowledge that your body possesses innate self-healing mechanisms. Understand the importance of supporting these mechanisms through lifestyle choices.

3. **Listening to Signals:** Realize the significance of tuning into your body's signals and sensations. Understand that these cues can guide you towards optimal health and well-being.

4. **Alignment with Nature:** Recognize the alignment between your body and the natural world. Understand that embracing nature's rhythms and principles can promote balance.

5. **Respecting Your Body:** Understand the importance of treating your body with respect and care. Recognize that nourishing your body is a form of self-love and empowerment.

Self Reflection Questions

Reflect on your perception of your body. How can you deepen your appreciation for its intelligent design and intricate systems?

_____

_____

_____

_____

_____

_____

_____

_____

_____

_____

_____

_____

_____

Consider your approach to health and healing. How can you actively support your body's self-healing mechanisms through your lifestyle choices?

_____

_____

_____

_____

_____

_____

_____

_____

_____

_____

_____

_____

_____

_____

Think about your connection to your body's signals. How can you enhance your awareness of these cues to make more informed decisions for your well-being?

_____

_____

_____

_____

_____

_____

_____

_____

_____

_____

_____

Reflect on the alignment between your body and nature. How can you incorporate nature's rhythms and principles into your daily life to promote balance and harmony?

_____

_____

_____

_____

_____

_____

_____

_____

_____

_____

_____

Consider your self-care practices. How can you approach your body with greater respect and care, recognizing that nurturing it is an act of self-love and empowerment?

Two Different Biopsychologies

Key Lessons

1. **Understanding Biopsychologies:** Recognize that every individual has two biopsychologies - the human and the spiritual. Understand that these aspects influence your thoughts, emotions, and behaviors.

2. **Human Biopsychology:** Acknowledge that the human biopsychology is based on conditioning, fears, and societal norms. Understand that it can lead to pain and suffering when not examined.

3. **Spiritual Biopsychology:** Realize that the spiritual biopsychology is rooted in consciousness and higher truths. Understand that aligning with this aspect can lead to inner peace and liberation.

4. **The Dance Between Two:** Recognize the interplay between the human and spiritual biopsychologies. Understand that awareness of this dance is essential for growth and transformation.

5. **Choosing Your Focus:** Understand that you have the power to choose which biopsychology to emphasize. Recognize that shifting towards your spiritual aspect can lead to radical awakening.

Self Reflection Questions

Reflect on your biopsychologies. How can you recognize the influence of both the human and spiritual aspects in shaping your thoughts and behaviors?

_____

_____

_____

_____

_____

_____

_____

_____

_____

_____

_____

_____

_____

Consider your conditioned responses. How can you become aware of your human biopsychology's conditioning and fears that contribute to pain?

_____

_____

_____

_____

_____

_____

_____

_____

_____

_____

_____

_____

_____

_____

Think about your connection to higher truths. How can you align with your spiritual biopsychology to cultivate inner peace and liberation?

_____

_____

_____

_____

_____

_____

_____

_____

_____

_____

_____

_____

_____

Reflect on the interplay between your biopsychologies.
How can you actively observe and navigate the dance
between your human and spiritual aspects?

_____

_____

_____

_____

_____

_____

_____

_____

_____

_____

_____

_____

Consider your focus in daily life. How can you choose to
emphasize your spiritual biopsychology, leading you
towards a path of radical awakening and empowerment?

Part Four: CRACKING THE MATRIX
Fact or Fiction?

Key Lessons

1. **Questioning Beliefs:** Understand the importance of questioning your beliefs and assumptions. Recognize that not all beliefs are based on truth or reality.

2. **Uncovering Untruths:** Acknowledge that many beliefs are based on conditioning, fears, and societal norms. Understand that uncovering these untruths is essential for personal growth.

3. **Discerning Truth:** Realize the significance of discerning between factual truths and perceived truths. Understand that the truth often lies beyond surface appearances.

4. **Challenging Narrative:** Recognize the power of challenging the narratives you've internalized. Understand that doing so can lead to liberation from limiting beliefs.

5. **Your Inner Observer:** Understand that you have an inner observer that can discern fact from fiction. Recognize the importance of cultivating this awareness.

Self Reflection Questions

Reflect on your beliefs. How can you actively question and examine them to determine if they align with truth or if they are based on conditioning?

_____

_____

_____

_____

_____

_____

_____

_____

_____

_____

_____

_____

_____

Consider the source of your beliefs. How can you uncover the untruths that may have been shaped by fears or societal norms?

_____

_____

_____

_____

_____

_____

_____

_____

_____

_____

_____

_____

_____

_____

_____

Think about your perception of truth. How can you hone your ability to discern factual truth from perceived truth in various situations?

_____

_____

_____

_____

_____

_____

_____

_____

_____

_____

_____

———————————————————

———————

Reflect on your internal narratives. How can you challenge these narratives to break free from limiting beliefs and experiences of pain?

———————————————————

———————————————————

———————————————————

———————————————————

———————————————————

———————————————————

———————————————————

———————————————————

———————————————————

———————————————————

———————————————————

———————

Consider your awareness of inner observation. How can you cultivate and trust this inner observer to guide you in differentiating between fact and fiction?

The Lies About Love

Key Lessons

1. **Misconceptions about Love:** Understand that society often perpetuates unrealistic notions of love. Recognize that these misconceptions can lead to pain and unfulfillment.

2. **Dependency vs. Love:** Acknowledge the difference between genuine love and dependency. Understand that true love is not based on needing someone for validation or security.

3. **Self-Love:** Realize that love begins with self-love. Understand that loving yourself fully is essential before seeking love from others.

4. **Unconditional Love:** Recognize that love should not be based on conditions or expectations. Understand that practicing unconditional love brings freedom and authenticity.

5. **Love as Liberation:** Understand that true love liberates rather than confines. Recognize that embracing a healthy understanding of love empowers you to live authentically.

Self Reflection Questions

Reflect on your beliefs about love. How can you identify and challenge societal misconceptions that may have influenced your understanding of love?

_____

_____

_____

_____

_____

_____

_____

_____

_____

_____

_____

_____

Consider your relationships. How can you differentiate between genuine love and unhealthy dependency in your interactions with others?

_____

_____

_____

_____

_____

_____

_____

_____

_____

_____

_____

_____

_____

_____

_____

Think about your self-love journey. How can you prioritize loving and accepting yourself fully before seeking love from external sources?

_____

_____

_____

_____

_____

_____

_____

_____

_____

_____

_____

_____

—————————

—————

Reflect on conditions in your relationships. How can you shift towards practicing unconditional love, free from expectations and limitations?

—————————
—————————
—————————
—————————
—————————
—————————
—————————
—————————
—————————
—————————
—————————

—————

Consider your perception of love's impact. How can you embrace a perspective that views love as liberating, enabling you to live a life of authenticity and empowerment?

The Lies About Marriage and Divorce

Key Lessons

1. **Challenging Unrealistic Expectations:** Understand that societal ideals about marriage may not reflect reality. Recognize the importance of challenging unrealistic expectations.

2. **Authentic Partnership:** Acknowledge that a healthy marriage is built on genuine partnership. Understand that mutual respect, communication, and support are fundamental.

3. **Personal Growth in Marriage:** Realize that marriage can be a catalyst for personal growth. Understand that facing challenges together can lead to transformation and deeper connection.

4. **Divorce as Empowerment:** Recognize that divorce is not a failure but an opportunity for growth. Understand that it's a step towards reclaiming your authentic self and happiness.

5. **Self-Love in Marriage and Divorce:** Understand that self-love is essential in both marriage and divorce. Recognize that honoring your needs and boundaries is a form of empowerment.

Self Reflection Questions

Reflect on your beliefs about marriage. How can you challenge societal ideals and expectations to create a realistic and fulfilling understanding of marriage?

_____

_____

_____

_____

_____

_____

_____

_____

_____

_____

_____

_____

_____

Consider your partnership. How can you ensure that your marriage is built on authentic partnership, characterized by mutual respect and open communication?

_____

_____

_____

_____

_____

_____

_____

_____

_____

_____

_____

_____

_____

_____

_____

Think about challenges in your marriage. How can you view them as opportunities for personal growth and transformation, both individually and as a couple?

_____

_____

_____

_____

_____

_____

_____

_____

_____

_____

_____

_____

_____

_____

Reflect on your perception of divorce. How can you shift towards viewing divorce as a step towards empowerment and a chance to reclaim your happiness?

_____
_____
_____
_____
_____
_____
_____
_____
_____
_____
_____
_____

_____

Consider your approach to self-love. How can you prioritize self-love both within a marriage and during divorce, honoring your needs and boundaries along the way?

Part Five: AWAKENING FROM THE MATRIX
Embracing Fearless Boundaries

Key Lessons

1. **Boundary Definition:** Understand the importance of defining clear boundaries in your life. Recognize that boundaries protect your well-being and preserve your authenticity.

2. **Honoring Your Needs:** Acknowledge that setting boundaries means prioritizing your needs and values. Understand that you have the right to advocate for yourself.

3. **Saying No:** Realize that saying "no" is a powerful act of self-respect. Understand that you don't have to please others at the expense of your own comfort.

4. **Boundary-Respecting Relationships:** Recognize that healthy relationships respect your boundaries. Understand that those who truly care about you will honor your limits.

5. **Empowerment Through Boundaries:** Understand that setting and maintaining boundaries empowers you to live authentically and fearlessly. Recognize that it's a step towards self-empowerment.

Self Reflection Questions

Reflect on your boundaries. How can you actively define and communicate your boundaries to protect your well-being and authenticity?

_____

_____

_____

_____

_____

_____

_____

_____

_____

_____

_____

Consider your needs and values. How can you prioritize these by setting boundaries, ensuring your own well-being remains at the forefront?

_____

_____

_____

_____

_____

_____

_____

_____

_____

_____

_____

_____

_____

Think about saying "no." How can you shift towards viewing this as an act of self-respect rather than as a form of disappointing others?

_____

_____

_____

_____

_____

_____

_____

_____

_____

_____

_____

Reflect on your relationships. How can you identify and nurture connections that respect your boundaries, enhancing your sense of well-being?

_____

_____

_____

_____

_____

_____

_____

_____

_____

_____

_____

Consider your journey towards empowerment. How can you embrace the idea that boundaries empower you to live fearlessly and authentically, aligned with your truth?

Embracing Sovereignty

Key Lessons

1. **Claiming Your Power:** Understand that embracing sovereignty means claiming your power and autonomy. Recognize that you have the ability to shape your life's direction.

2. **Personal Responsibility:** Acknowledge that sovereignty involves taking responsibility for your choices and actions. Understand that this accountability empowers you to create change.

3. **Authentic Decision-Making:** Realize that sovereignty allows you to make decisions aligned with your truth. Understand that by doing so, you can live a life of authenticity.

4. **Releasing External Validation:** Recognize that true sovereignty involves releasing the need for constant external validation. Comprehend that your value comes from the inside.

5. **Living Free:** Understand that embracing sovereignty leads to a life of freedom. Recognize that by owning your choices and authenticity, you break free from limitations.

Self Reflection Questions

Reflect on your sense of power. How can you actively claim your sovereignty and harness your power to shape the direction of your life?

_____

_____

_____

_____

_____

_____

_____

_____

_____

_____

_____

_____

_____

Consider your accountability. How can you take responsibility for your choices and actions, recognizing that your empowerment lies in this ownership?

_____

_____

_____

_____

_____

_____

_____

_____

_____

_____

_____

_____

_____

_____

Think about decision-making. How can you prioritize making choices that resonate with your truth and authenticity, embracing your sovereignty?

_____

_____

_____

_____

_____

_____

_____

_____

_____

_____

_____

_____

———————————————

———————

Reflect on validation-seeking behaviors. How can you shift towards recognizing your worth from within, rather than relying on external validation?

———————————————
———————————————
———————————————
———————————————
———————————————
———————————————
———————————————
———————————————
———————————————
———————————————

———————

Consider your perception of freedom. How can you embrace sovereignty to break free from limitations and live a life of authenticity and empowerment?

Embracing Accountability

Key Lessons

1. **Personal Responsibility:** Understand that embracing accountability means taking ownership of your actions, choices, and their outcomes. Recognize that you play a crucial role in shaping your life.

2. **Learning from Mistakes:** Acknowledge that mistakes are opportunities for growth. Understand that accountability involves learning from your missteps and making amends.

3. **Empowerment Through Choice:** Realize that accountability empowers you to make conscious choices aligned with your values. Understand that this freedom enables you to live authentically.

4. **Breaking Patterns:** Recognize that embracing accountability helps you break free from recurring negative patterns. Understand that by taking control, you can create positive change.

5. **Shifting from Victimhood:** Understand that accountability requires shifting from a victim mentality to a position of power. Recognize that you have the ability to create change.

Self Reflection Questions

Reflect on your actions and choices. How can you actively take responsibility for them, recognizing your role in shaping the outcomes in your life?

_____

_____

_____

_____

_____

_____

_____

_____

_____

_____

_____

_____

_____

Consider your approach to mistakes. How can you embrace accountability as a means to learn, grow, and make amends when necessary?

_____

_____

_____

_____

_____

_____

_____

_____

_____

_____

_____

_____

_____

_____

Think about your decision-making. How can you use accountability to make conscious choices that align with your values and authenticity?

_____

_____

_____

_____

_____

_____

_____

_____

_____

_____

_____

———

Reflect on recurring patterns in your life. How can embracing accountability help you break free from these patterns and create positive change?

———

Consider your perspective on challenges. How can you shift from a victim mentality to one of empowerment and accountability, recognizing your ability to create change?

Final Self-Evaluation Questions

1. What was the key reason you bought this book?

_____

_____

_____

———

2. To what extent could you say you achieved your objectives?

_____

_____

_____

———

3. Following what you've learned, what actions/behaviours should you start taking/doing?

_____

_____

_____

_____

_____

4. What actions/behaviours should you stop doing?

_____

_____

_____

——

5. Do you think you could possibly improve following what
you learned from this book? What makes you think so?

_____

_____

_____

_____

_____

_____

————